KU-432-790

The Lincoln Memorial

by Frances E. Ruffin

Reading consultant: Susan Nations, M.Ed., author/literacy coach/consultant in literacy development

WEEKLY WR READER®
EARLY LEARNING LIBRARY

Please visit our web site at: www.earlyliteracy.cc
For a free color catalog describing Weekly Reader® Early Learning Library's
list of high-quality books, call 1-877-445-5824 (USA) or 1-800-387-3178 (Canada).
Weekly Reader® Early Learning Library's fax: (414) 336-0164.

Library of Congress Cataloging-in-Publication Data

Ruffin, Frances E.
    The Lincoln Memorial / by Frances E. Ruffin.
      p. cm. — (Places in American history)
    Includes bibliographical references and index.
    ISBN 0-8368-6411-5 (lib. bdg.)
    ISBN 0-8368-6418-2 (softcover)
    1. Lincoln Memorial (Washington, D.C.)—Juvenile literature. 2. Lincoln, Abraham, 1809–1865—
Monuments—Washington (D.C.)—Juvenile literature. 3. Washington (D.C.)—Buildings, structures,
etc.—Juvenile literature. I. Title.
    F203.4.L73R84 2006
    975.3—dc22
                                                        2005026266

This edition first published in 2006 by
Weekly Reader® Early Learning Library
A Member of the WRC Media Family of Companies
330 West Olive Street, Suite 100
Milwaukee, WI 53212 USA

Copyright © 2006 by Weekly Reader® Early Learning Library

Managing Editor: Valerie J. Weber
Editor: Barbara Kiely Miller
Art direction: Tammy West
Graphic design: Dave Kowalski
Photo research: Diane Laska-Swanke

Photo credits: Cover title, © Corel; pp. 4, 13, 18 © Mae Scanlan; p. 5 © Library of Congress/Getty Images;
p. 6 © North Wind Picture Archives; p. 7 © Hulton Archive/Getty Images; pp. 8, 20 © Bob Gomel/Time &
Life Pictures/Getty Images; p. 9 © MPI/Getty Images; pp. 10-11 Dave Kowalski/© Weekly Reader Early
Learning Library, 2006; pp. 12, 15, 16 © Library of Congress; p. 14 © Gibson Stock Photography; p. 19
© General Photographic Agency/Getty Images; p. 21 © Orlando/Hulton Archive/Getty Images

All rights reserved. No part of this book may be reproduced, stored in a retrieval system,
or transmitted in any form or by any means, electronic, mechanical, photocopying, recording,
or otherwise, without the prior written permission of the copyright holder.

Printed in the United States of America

1 2 3 4 5 6 7 8 9 10 09 08 07 06

Table of Contents

People can visit the Lincoln Memorial at night. The memorial is as beautiful after dark as it is during the day.

Honoring Abraham Lincoln

The Lincoln Memorial is in Washington, D.C. It is one of the most beautiful buildings in our nation's capital. The memorial was built to honor Abraham Lincoln. He was the sixteenth president of the United States.

Abraham Lincoln was president from 1861 to 1865. During that time, states in the North and states in the South fought each other. Their fight was called the Civil War.

During the Civil War, President Lincoln gave a famous speech in Gettysburg, Pennsylvania.

Millions of African Americans were slaves before
the Civil War.

The states were fighting over whether white people
should own black people as slaves. Slaves had to
work hard without getting paid. They were not free
to live where or how they wanted. The states in the
South wanted to keep slavery. President Lincoln
and the states in the North wanted to end slavery.

On January 1, 1863, Abraham Lincoln signed an important paper. The paper said slaves in the South were free! The North and the South still fought, however. Two years later, the Civil War ended. Slavery in the United States was over!

President Lincoln's top helpers in the government watched him work on the paper that would free slaves.

A President Is Killed

Not everyone liked or agreed with President Lincoln. On April 14, 1865, Lincoln went to a theater to watch a play. He sat in a box of seats high above the stage. A man shot Lincoln from behind. The man jumped onto the stage to escape. The president died the next morning at a nearby house.

President Lincoln was sitting here at Ford's Theatre when he was shot.

Most Americans were sad about Lincoln's death. Leaders in government wanted to build a memorial. The building would honor President Lincoln. It would remind people that Lincoln was a great president. The government, however, did not have money then to build the memorial.

People lined up to watch as the president's body was carried through the streets of Washington, D.C.

Planning a Memorial

In 1911, Congress passed a law to build a memorial to President Lincoln. They agreed to spend two million dollars. A group formed to choose the kind of memorial to build. They decided to build it on

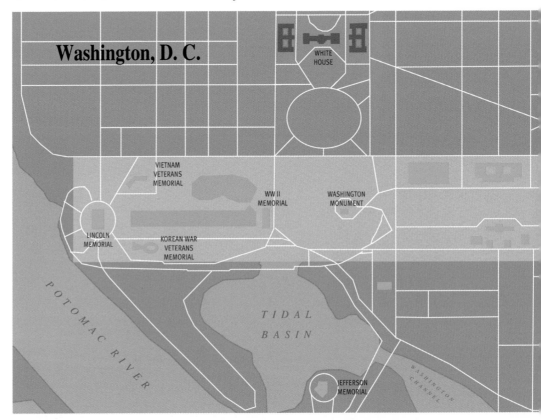

Washington, D. C.

WHITE HOUSE

VIETNAM VETERANS MEMORIAL

WW II MEMORIAL

WASHINGTON MONUMENT

LINCOLN MEMORIAL

KOREAN WAR VETERANS MEMORIAL

POTOMAC RIVER

TIDAL BASIN

JEFFERSON MEMORIAL

WASHINGTON CHANNEL

the west end of the National Mall. The National Mall is a long park in Washington, D.C. Important government buildings, memorials, and museums surround the Mall.

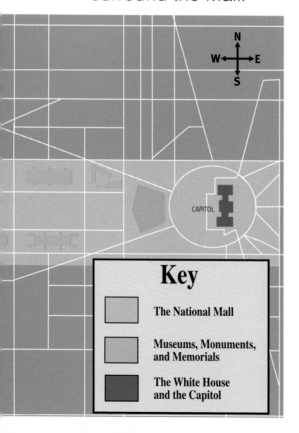

CAPITOL

Key

The National Mall

Museums, Monuments, and Memorials

The White House and the Capitol

The National Mall has huge lawns and open spaces. Some people call it the nation's "front yard."

The Lincoln Memorial was built on ground that had once been a swamp.

Henry Bacon came up with the design. Building began in February 1914. The memorial was built with marble from Colorado, Tennessee, and Alabama. Limestone from Indiana was used, too. Fifty-six marble stairs lead up all four sides of the memorial. Thirty-six columns surround the memorial at the top of these stairs. The columns stand for the number of states in the country when Lincoln died.

Inside the memorial is a huge statue of Abraham Lincoln. Artist Daniel Chester French carved the statue from white marble from Georgia. French made Lincoln's face look like he was deep in thought.

The left hand in Lincoln's statue is closed to show his strength. The right hand is open to show his kindness.

IN THIS TEMPLE
AS IN THE HEARTS OF THE PEOPLE
FOR WHOM HE SAVED THE UNION
THE MEMORY OF ABRAHAM LINCOLN
IS ENSHRINED FOREVER

The seated statue of Lincoln faces a pool on the National Mall. The Washington Monument stands at the other end of the pool. This tall tower honors George Washington. He was the country's first president. Behind the Washington Monument stands the Capitol. Members of Congress work in this important building.

From the memorial's top step, people can see this view of the Washington Monument.

The Memorial Opens

Building the Lincoln Memorial took eight years. It opened on Memorial Day, May 30, 1922. Memorial Day is the holiday when we remember people who died fighting for our country.

President Warren G. Harding spoke at the opening of the Lincoln Memorial.

Thousands of people came to honor President
Lincoln when his memorial opened.

More than fifty thousand people came to celebrate
the completion of the Lincoln Memorial. Robert
Lincoln was one of them. He was the only living
son of President Lincoln. Hundreds of people who
had fought in the Civil War also came.

Visiting the Lincoln Memorial

Visitors to the Lincoln Memorial must walk up the steep steps to the opening at the front. The inside of the memorial is divided into three sections called chambers. Tall, wide columns separate the chambers. Visitors enter the largest chamber at the center of the memorial. It holds the statue of President Lincoln.

Lincoln Memorial Facts

Lincoln's statue was carved from twenty-eight pieces of white marble. The pieces were put together like a giant puzzle.

Lincoln's statue is 19 feet (6 meters) tall. If the statue could stand up, Lincoln would be 28 feet (9 m) tall!

The names of the states are carved above the columns on the outside of the memorial.

The back of the Lincoln penny and the five-dollar bill both show President Abraham Lincoln seated in his memorial.

FOUR SCORE AND SEVEN YEARS AGO OUR FATHERS BROUGHT FORTH ON THIS CONTINENT A NEW NATION CONCEIVED IN LIBERTY AND DEDICATED TO THE PROPOSITION THAT ALL MEN ARE CREATED EQUAL · NOW WE ARE ENGAGED IN A GREAT CIVIL WAR TESTING WHETHER THAT NATION OR ANY NATION SO CONCEIVED AND SO DEDICATED CAN LONG ENDURE · WE ARE MET ON A GREAT BATTLEFIELD OF THAT WAR · WE HAVE COME TO DEDICATE A PORTION OF THAT FIELD AS A FINAL RESTING PLACE FOR THOSE WHO HERE GAVE THEIR LIVES THAT THAT NATION MIGHT LIVE · IT IS ALTOGETHER FITTING AND PROPER THAT WE SHOULD DO THIS · BUT IN A LARGER SENSE WE CAN NOT DEDICATE~WE CAN NOT CONSECRATE~WE CAN NOT HALLOW~ THIS GROUND · THE BRAVE MEN LIVING AND DEAD WHO STRUGGLED HERE HAVE CONSECRATED IT FAR ABOVE OUR POOR POWER TO ADD OR DETRACT · THE WORLD WILL LITTLE NOTE NOR LONG REMEMBER WHAT WE SAY HERE BUT IT CAN NEVER FORGET WHAT THEY DID HERE · IT IS FOR US THE LIVING RATHER TO BE DEDICATED HERE TO THE UNFINISHED WORK WHICH THEY WHO FOUGHT HERE HAVE THUS FAR SO NOBLY ADVANCED · IT IS RATHER FOR US TO BE HERE DEDICATED TO THE GREAT TASK REMAINING BEFORE US~ THAT FROM THESE HONORED DEAD WE TAKE INCREASED DEVOTION TO THAT CAUSE FOR WHICH THEY GAVE THE LAST FULL MEASURE OF DEVOTION~ THAT WE HERE HIGHLY RESOLVE THAT THESE DEAD SHALL NOT HAVE DIED IN VAIN~THAT THIS NATION UNDER GOD SHALL HAVE A NEW BIRTH OF FREEDOM~ AND THAT GOVERNMENT OF THE PEOPLE BY THE PEOPLE FOR THE PEOPLE SHALL NOT PERISH FROM THE EARTH ·

The Gettysburg Address is one of the most important speeches ever given by a president.

In another chamber, the words of the Gettysburg Address are carved on the walls. This address is a speech that Lincoln gave on November 19, 1863. His speech honored the men who had died in a huge battle in Gettysburg, Pennsylvania. It also reminded people that all men were created equal. A painting of the Angel of Truth hangs on the walls. It shows the angel freeing people who were slaves.

Another speech is carved into a wall in the third chamber. Lincoln gave this speech when he became president for the second time. In another painting, the Angel of Truth joins the hands of people from the North and the South. The painting shows a united nation.

In March 1865, Abraham Lincoln spoke after taking the oath as president for the second time. This speech is carved on a wall of the Lincoln Memorial.

The statue of Lincoln has watched over many important events. One of the largest was the March on Washington in August 1963. Thousands of people met in front of the Lincoln Memorial. They were there to fight for the rights of African Americans.

During the March on Washington, Martin Luther King, Jr., spoke from the Lincoln Memorial. A huge crowd heard his famous "I Have a Dream" speech.

The Lincoln Memorial reminds Americans what a great president Abraham Lincoln was. He led the United States when it was about to split apart. He helped it unite. He ended slavery. We are a nation of different people united together. The Lincoln Memorial stands to remind people that everyone is equal in the United States.

The statue of President Lincoln inspires visitors of all ages.

Glossary

carved — made an object or letters by cutting them into hard or soft materials

Civil War — the American war fought between Northern and Southern states, from 1861 to 1865

Congress — the part of the United States government that makes laws

inspires — fills with great emotion; moves to action

limestone — a rock that is formed mostly of crushed and tightly packed shells and coral

marble — a kind of limestone that can be highly polished

memorial — something that is used to remind us of people or events

oath — a promise that someone will do what he or she says or is telling the truth

slavery — when people are not free, are owned as property, and are made to work without pay

surround — to circle around on all sides

For More Information

Books

The Lincoln Memorial. National Landmarks (series).
   Kathleen W. Deady. (Putnam)

The Lincoln Memorial. American Symbols (series).
   Terri DeGezelle. (Capstone Press)

Lincoln Memorial. Pull Ahead Books (series).
   Kristin L. Nelson (Lerner Publishing)

The Lincoln Memorial. Let's See Library (series)
   Marc Tyler Nobleman (Compass Point Books)

Web Sites

The White House for Kids
http://www.whitehouse.gov/kids/presidents/
abrahamlincoln.html
Facts about Abraham Lincoln

Ben's Guide to the U.S. Government for Kids
http://bensguide.gpo.gov/3-5/symbols/lincoln.html
Read about many features of the Lincoln Memorial.

Index

About the Author

Frances E. Ruffin has written more than twenty-four books for children. She enjoys reading and writing about the lives of famous and ordinary people. She lives in New York City with her son, Timothy, a young writer who is writing his first novel.